My First Book Of Patterns

Pencil Control

With

This Book Belongs to

Wonder House

Standing Lines

Trace the dotted lines from top to bottom.

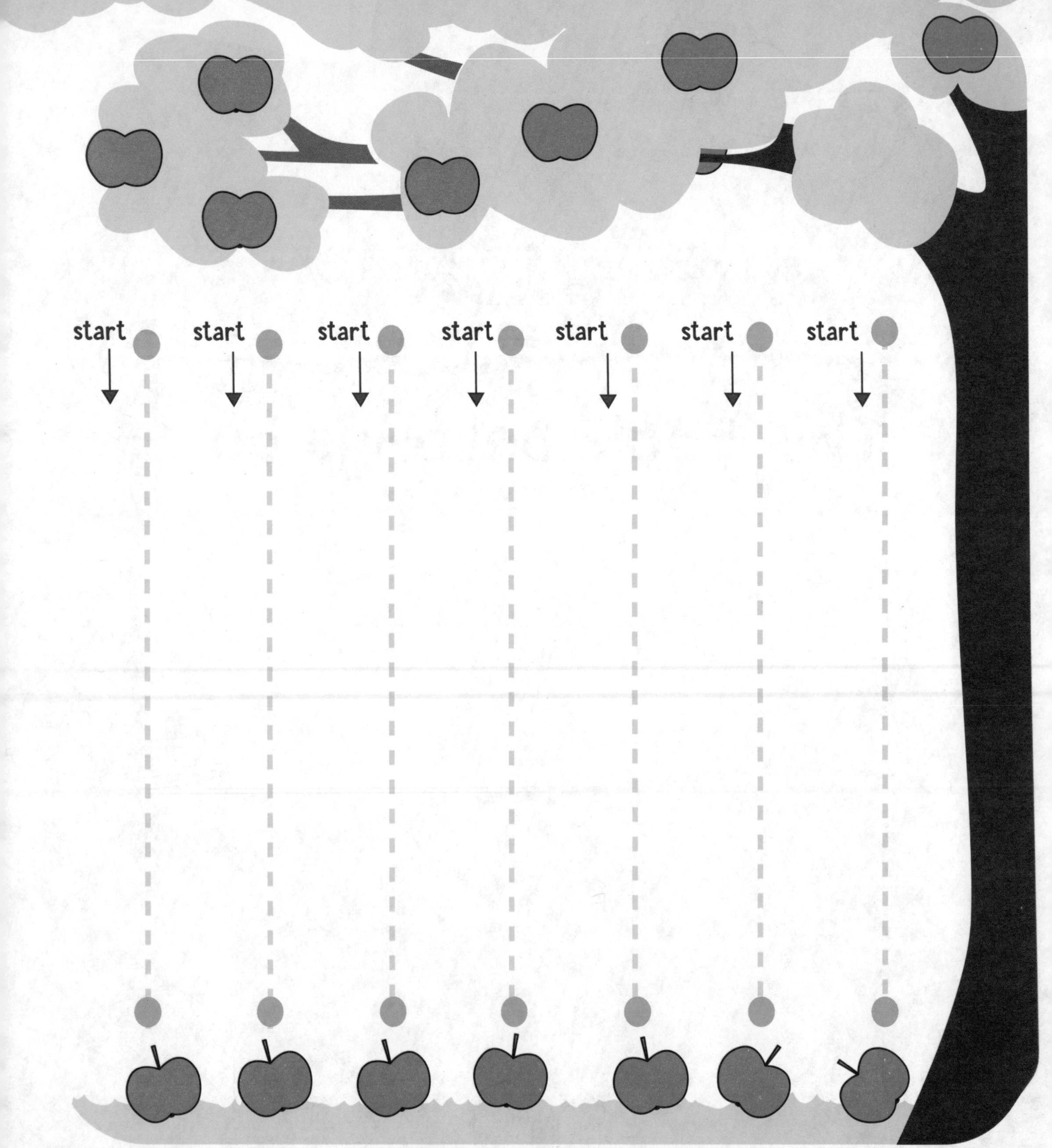

Sleeping Lines

Trace the dotted lines from left to right.

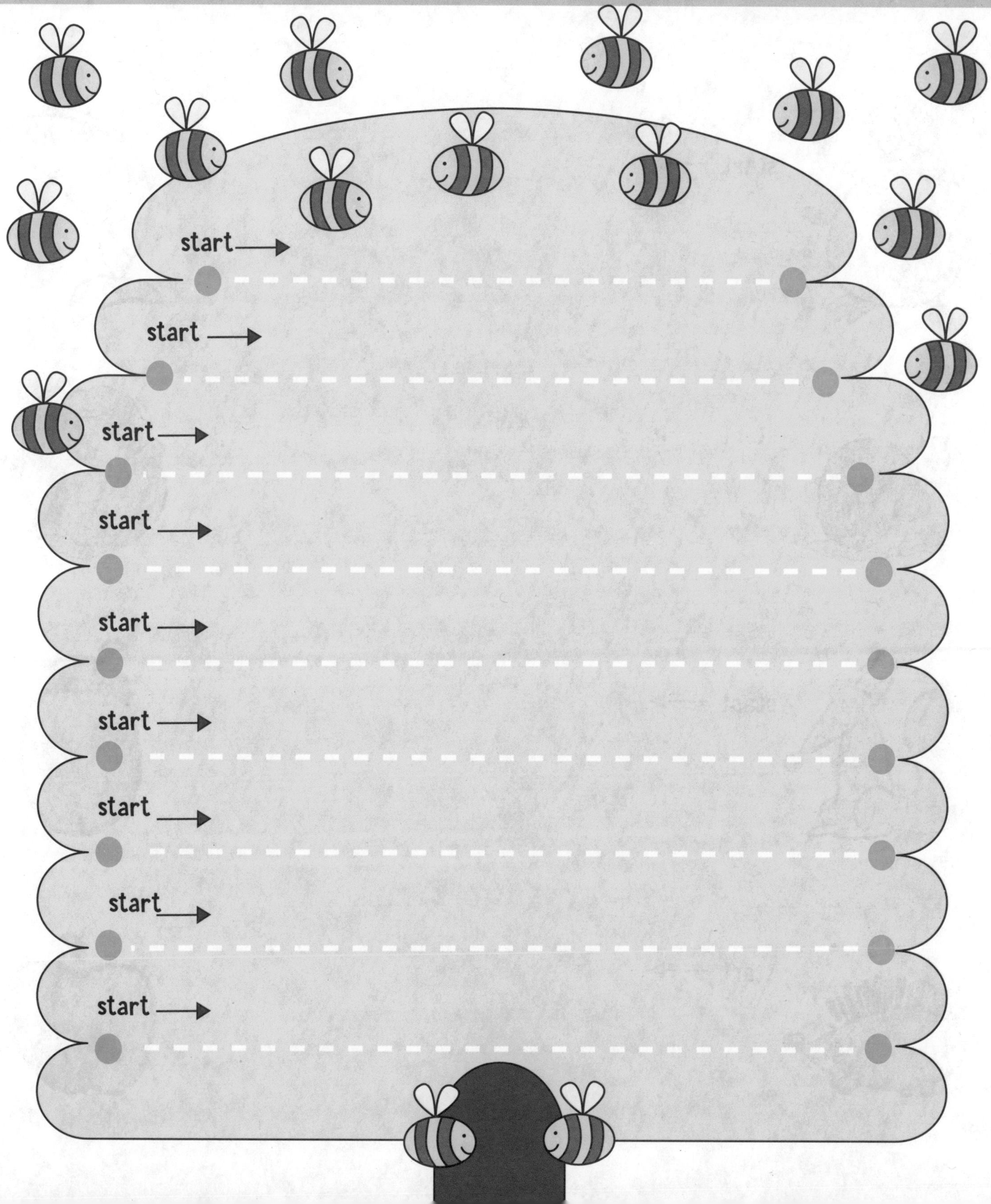

Food Search

Help the animals reach their favorite food by joining the dotted lines.

start →

start →

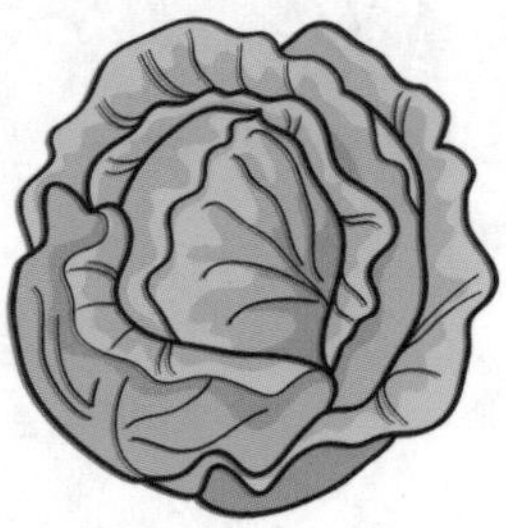

start →

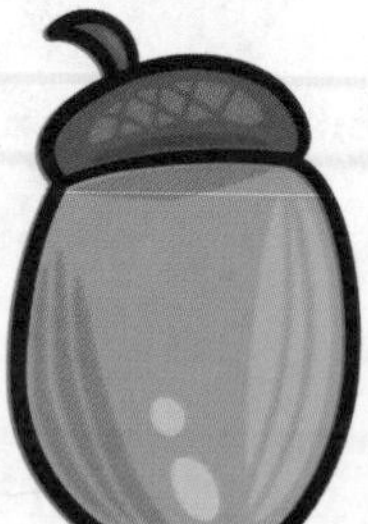

start →

Dog Path

Help the dog reach his home by drawing a line within the path given below.

Slanting Lines

Trace the dotted lines on the branch.

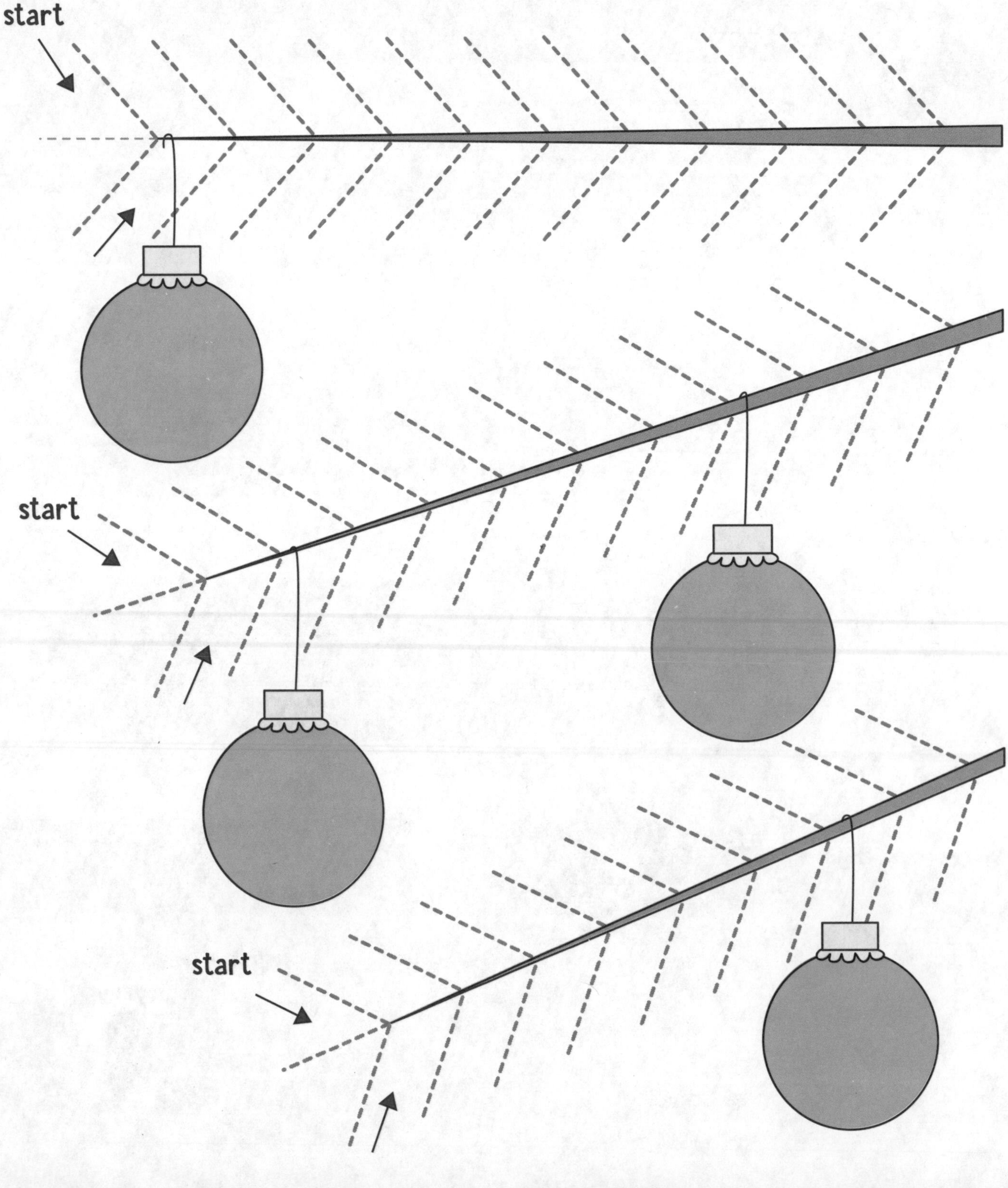

Zig-Zag Lines

Trace the dotted lines on the crocodile's back.

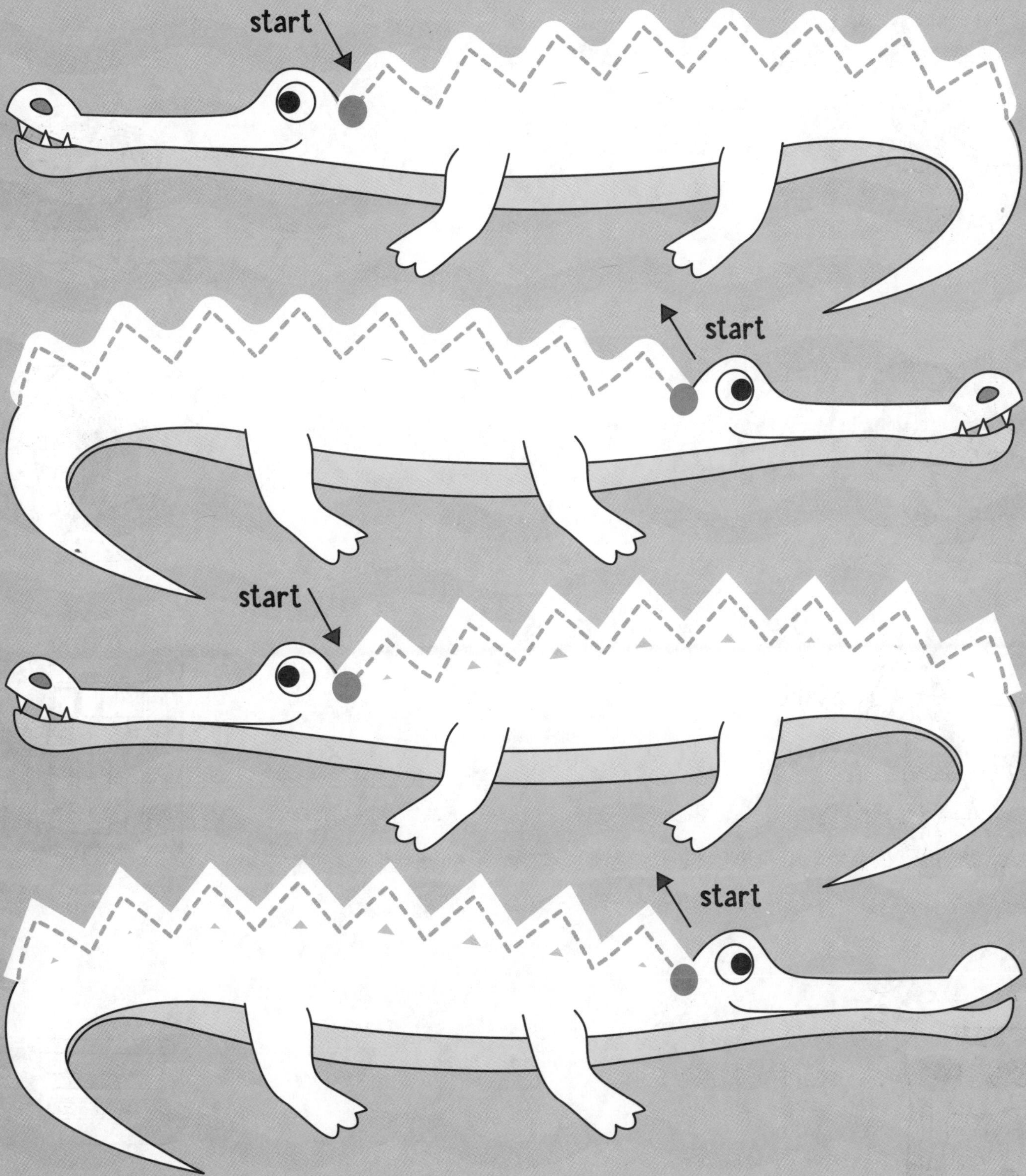

Way to Home

Trace the lines from the animals to their homes.

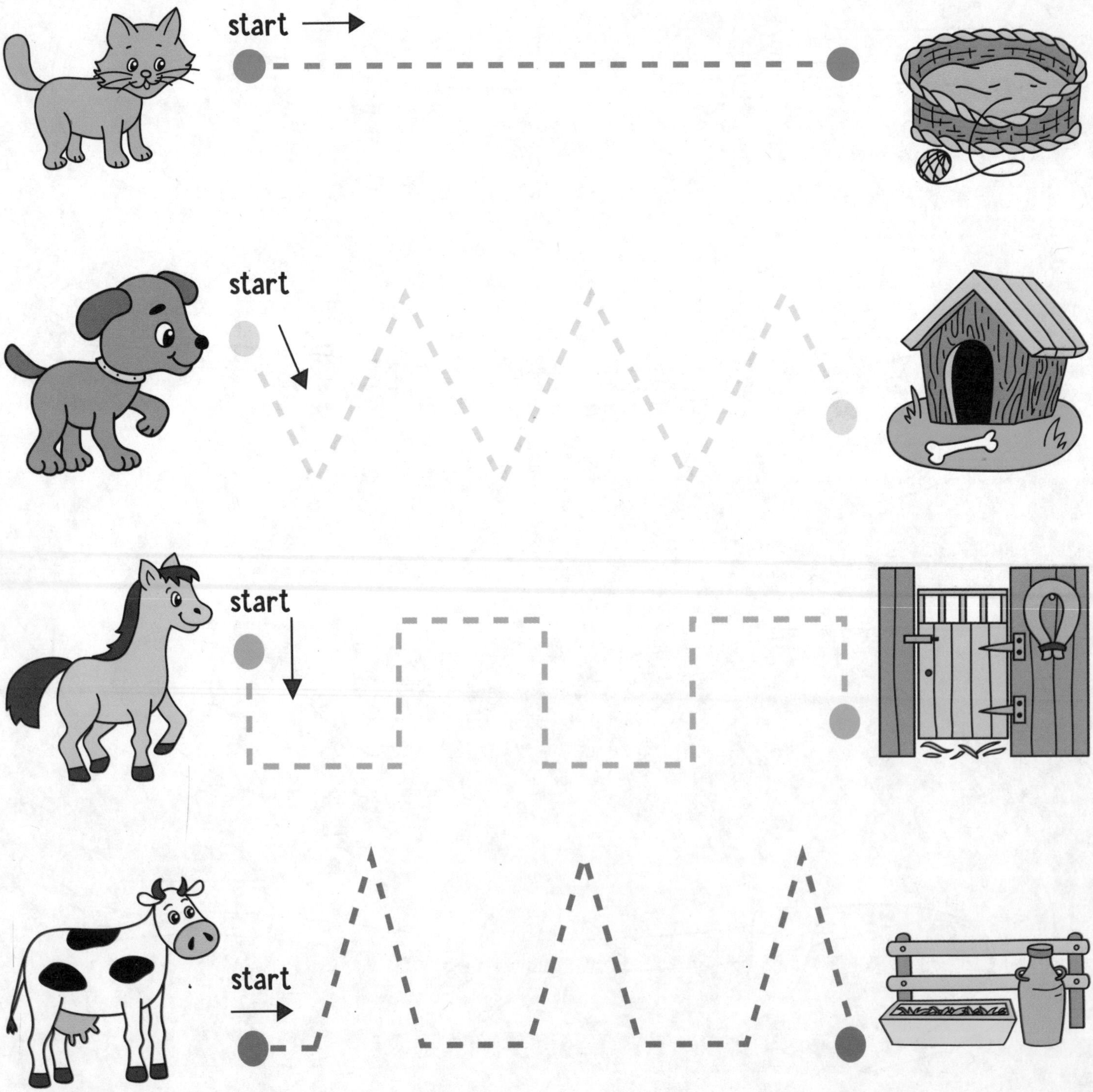

Friends Forever

Trace the dotted lines and help the friends meet.

Curved Lines

Trace the lines up and down. Help the ship reach the light house.

Wavy Lines

Trace the wavy lines to match the pictures.

Sailing Ship

Trace the dotted lines to finish the picture and then color it.

Curved Lines

Trace the dotted lines to complete the picture.

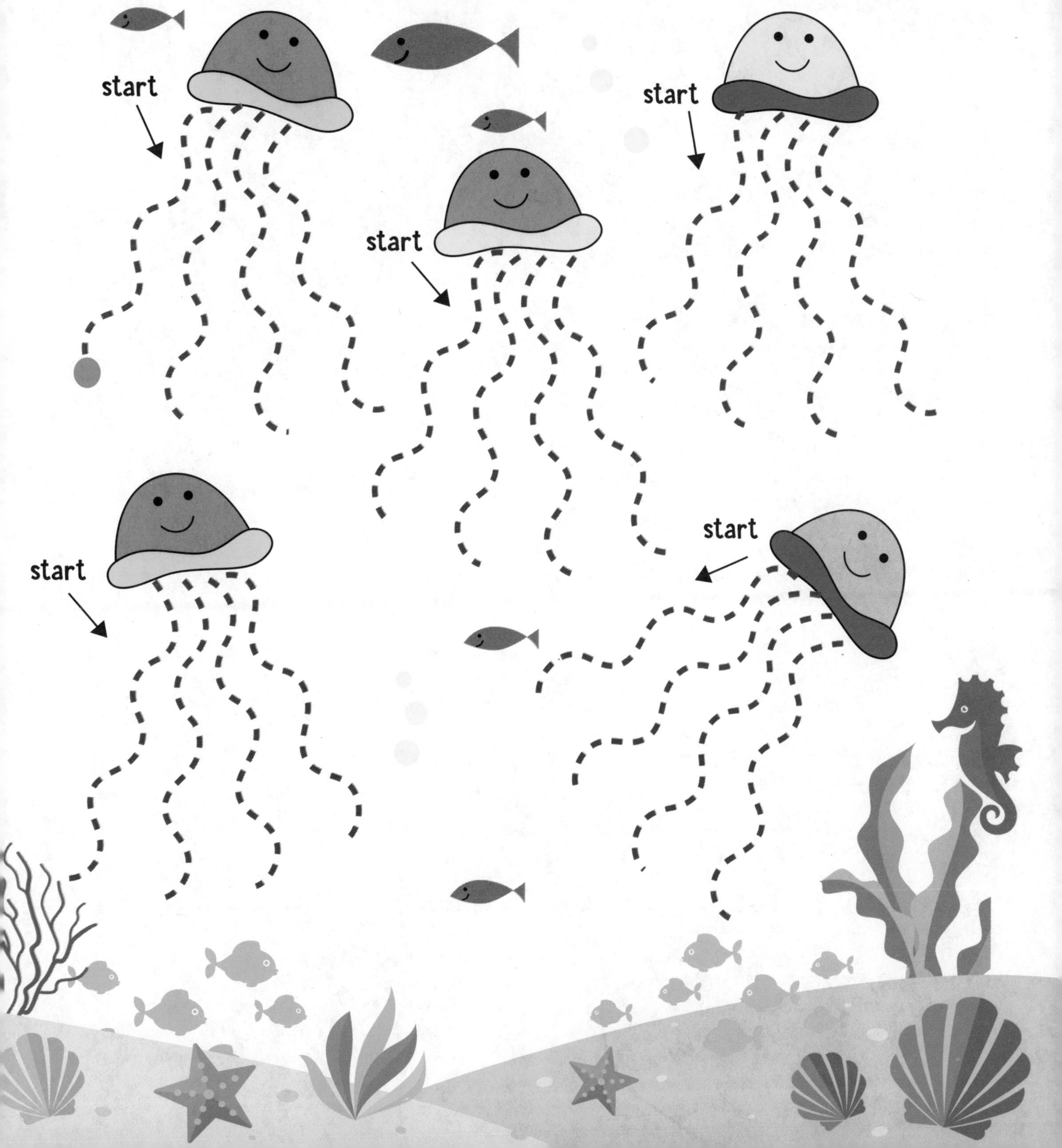

My House

Join the dots from 1 to 10 and color the house.

Ski Path

Trace the path taken by the tourist on the snow peak.

Autumn Foliage

Trace the path of the falling leaves and acorns.

Sunny Day

Trace the dotted lines to complete the sun's rays.

Lines and Vehicles

Trace the lines and match the vehicles.

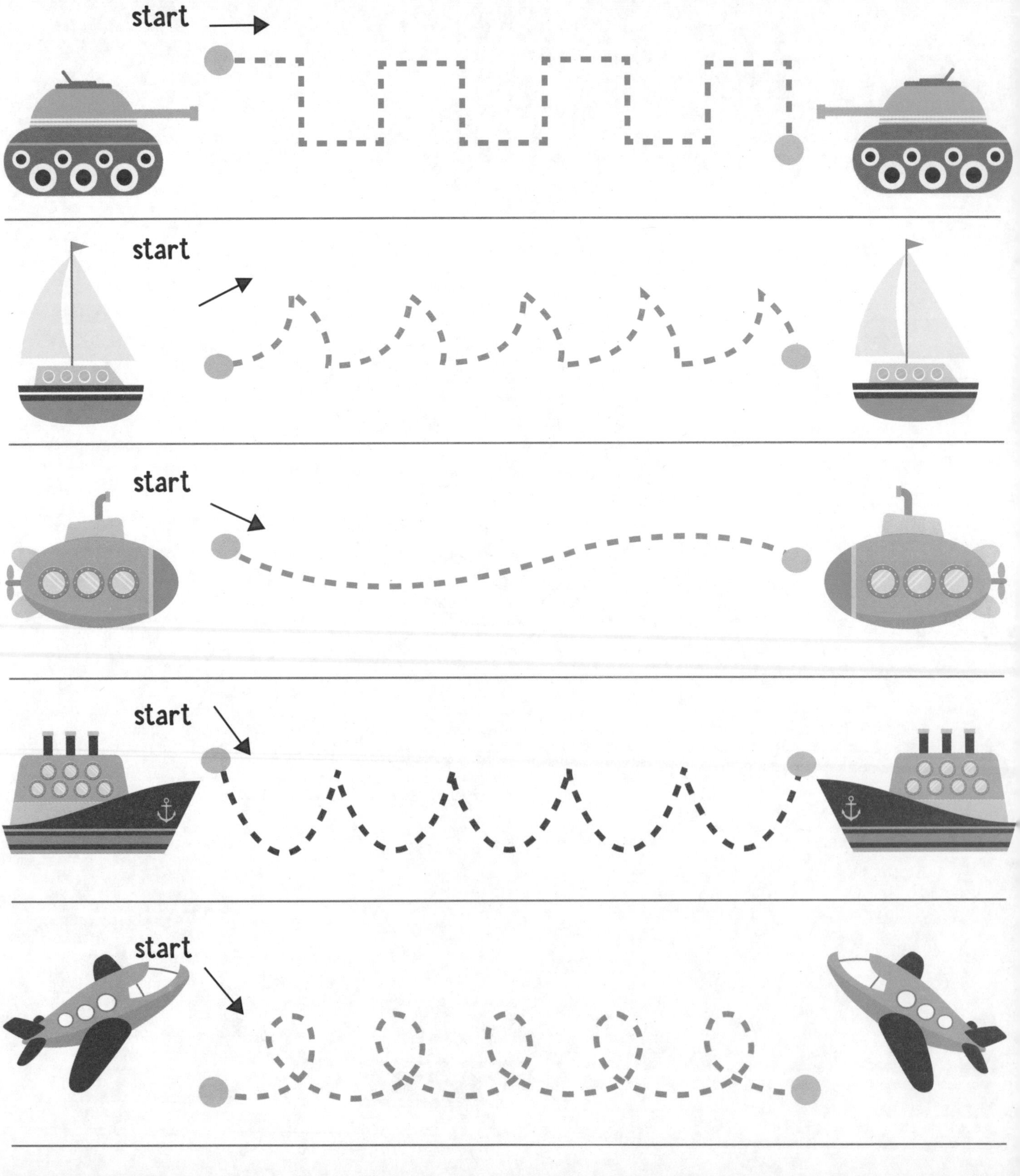

Busy Bees

Trace the lines and help the bees reach the flowers.

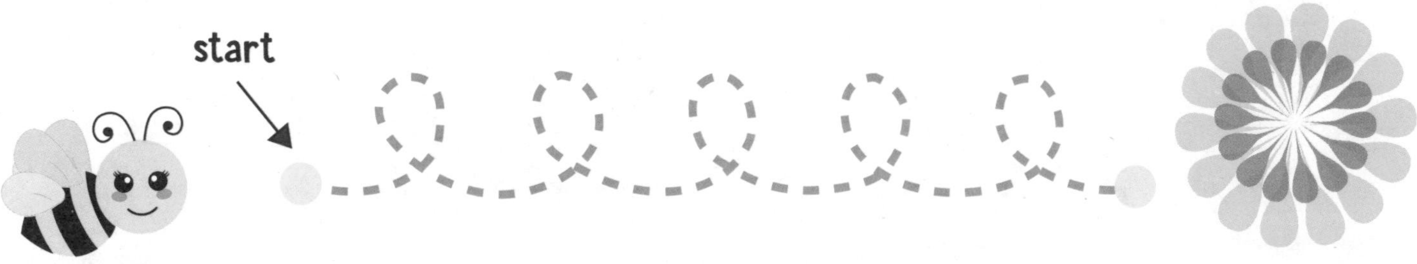

Spiral Patterns

Trace the spiral lines and complete the snails.

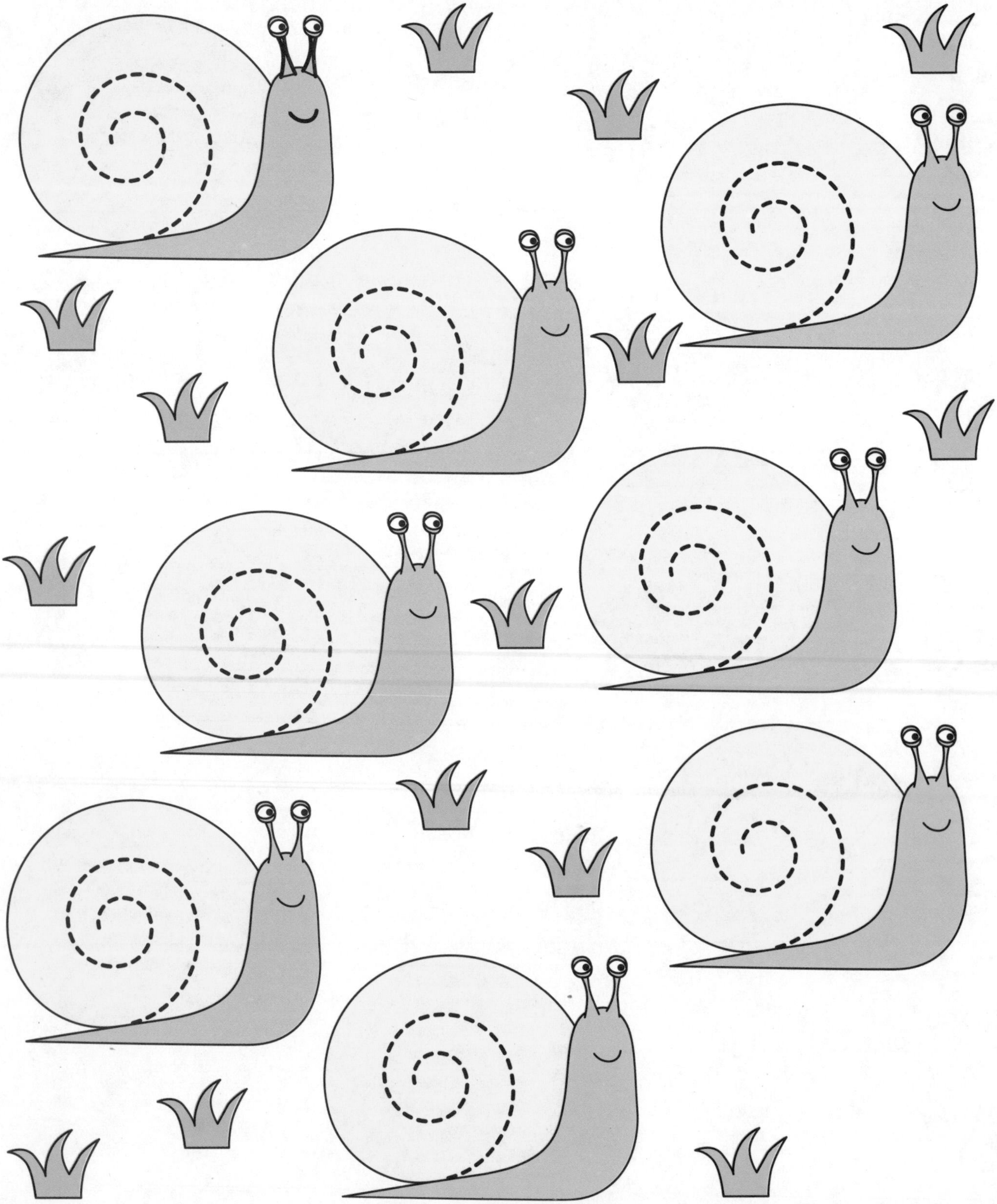

Candy Color

Trace the spiral lines and color the candies.

Blooming Tulips

Trace the spiral lines and color the tulips.

Join the Dots

Join the dots and complete the butterfly.

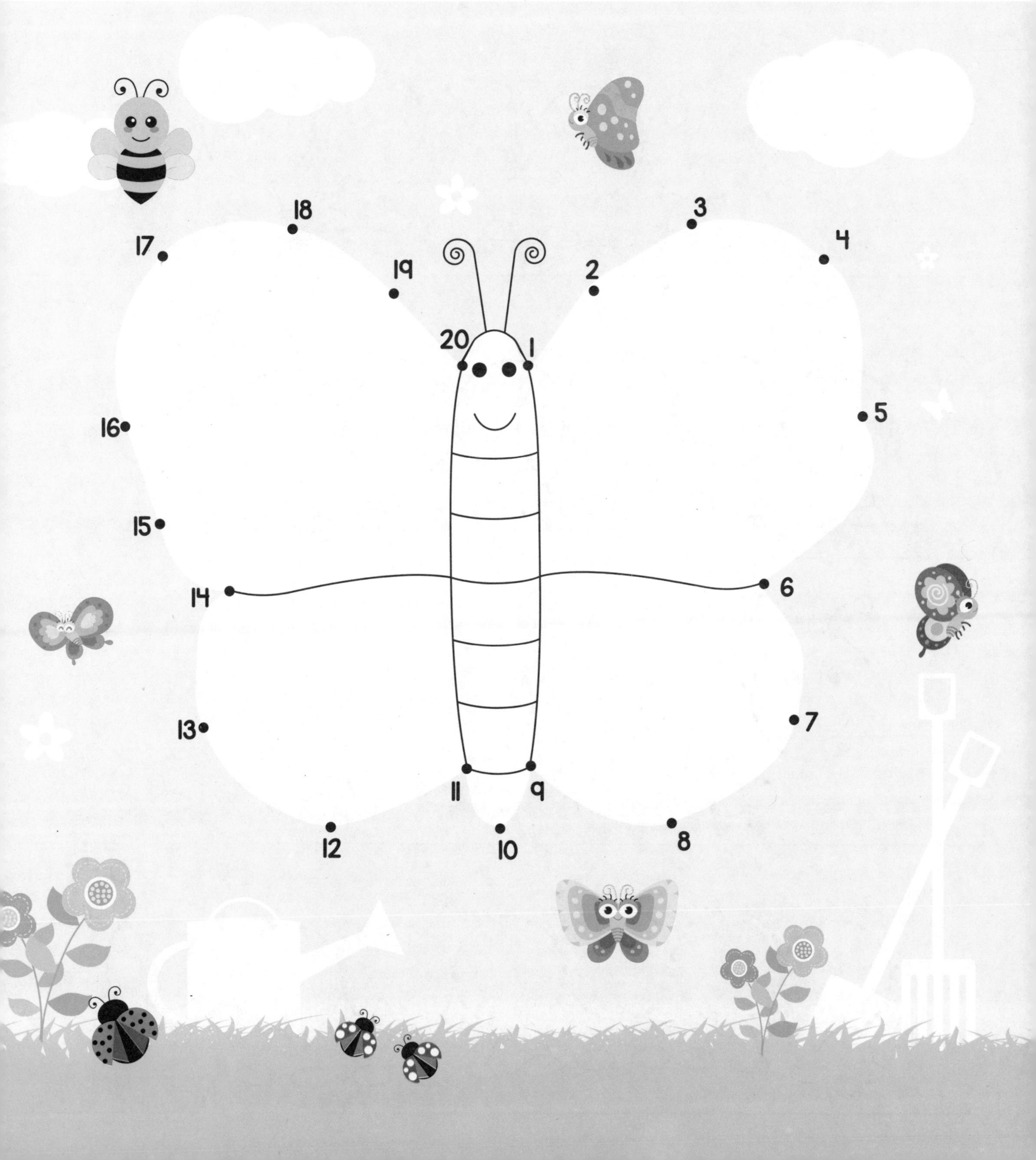

Caterpillars

Trace the circles and complete the caterpillars.

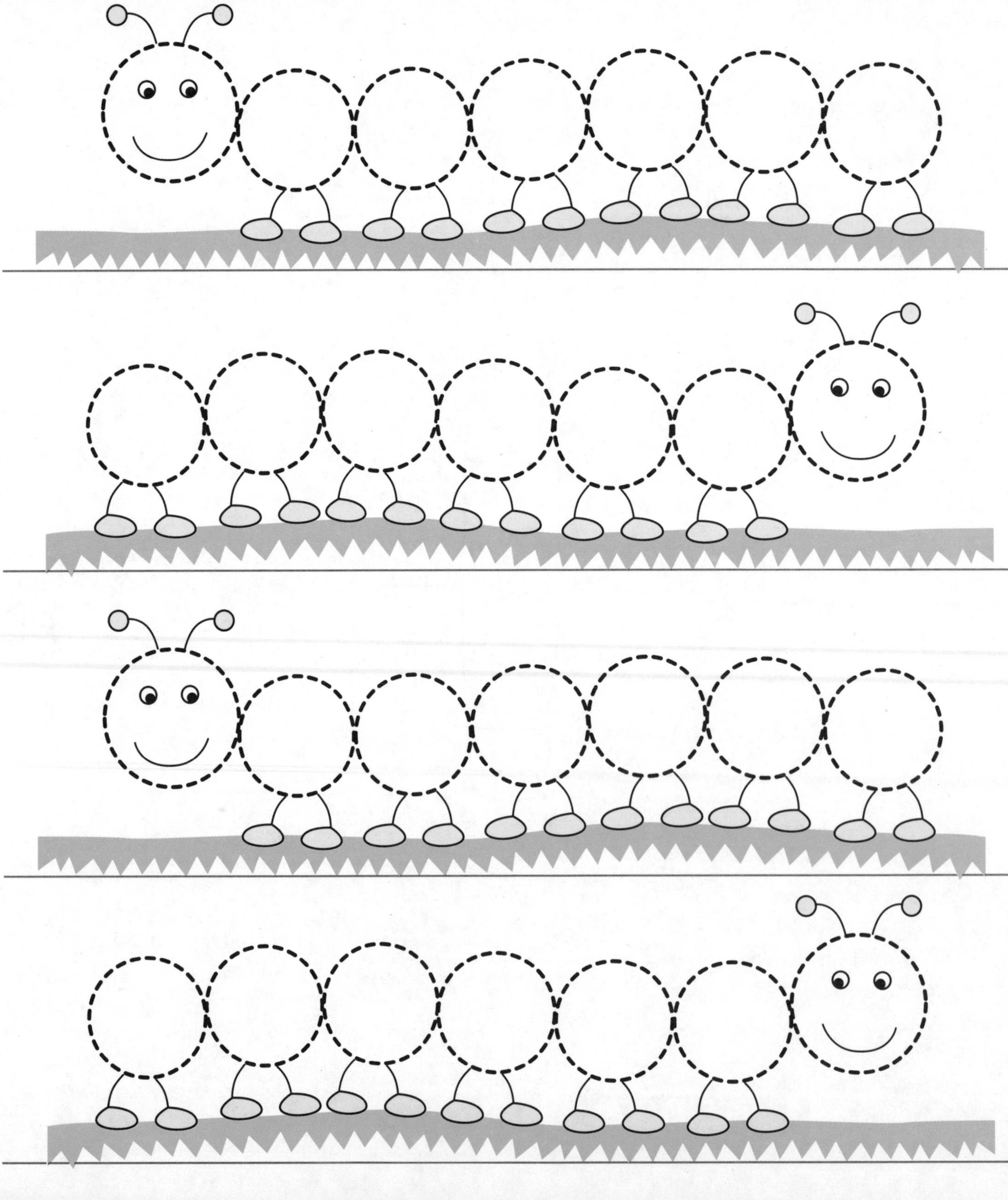

Ladybird

Trace the circles and color the ladybirds.

House and Windows

Trace the square windows and complete the house.

A Colorful Train

Trace the dotted lines and complete the train.

Stars

Trace the dotted lines and color to complete the stars.

Pine Trees

Trace the dotted lines and color to complete the trees.

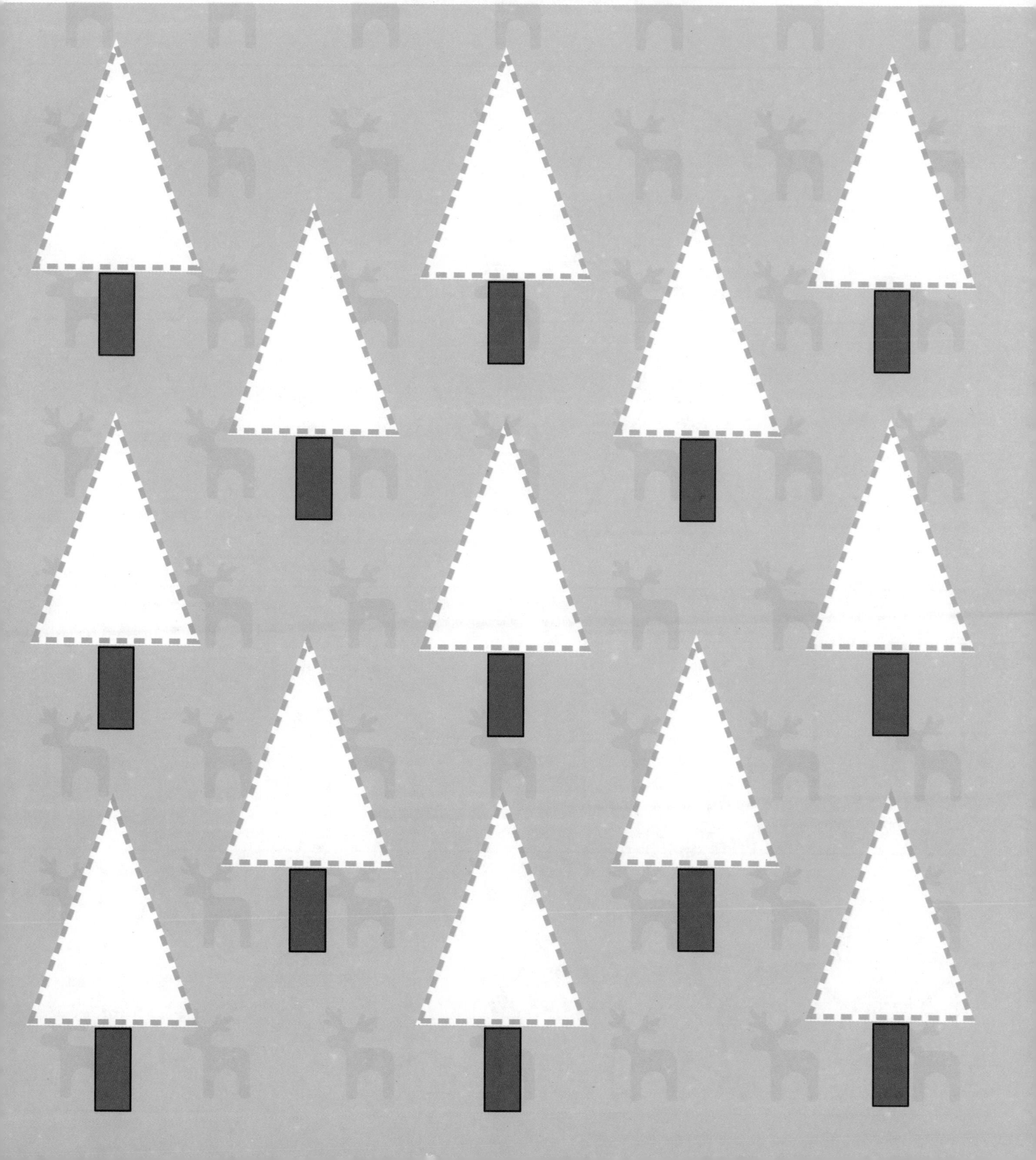

Basic Shapes

Trace the dotted lines and complete the patterns.

Halloween

Trace the dotted lines and color to complete the Halloween pumpkins.

Butterfly Park

Trace the dotted lines and color to complete the butterflies.

Fish Pond

Trace the dotted lines and color to complete the fish pattern.

Chef's Magic

Trace the dotted lines and complete the pattern.

Smoke Trail

Trace the dotted lines and complete the pattern.

Elephant Bath

Trace the dotted lines and help the elephant take a bath.

Spider Web

Trace the dotted lines and complete the web pattern.

Rainbow Colors

Trace the dotted lines and color the rainbow to complete the picture.

Light House

Trace the dotted lines to complete the pattern.

Merry Christmas!

Trace the dotted lines and color the stocking to complete the pattern.

X-mas Tree

Trace the dotted lines and color the tree.

Birthday Cake

Trace the dotted lines and color the candles to complete the lovely cake.

Yummy Ice Cream

Trace the dotted lines and color the ice cream to complete the tasty treat.

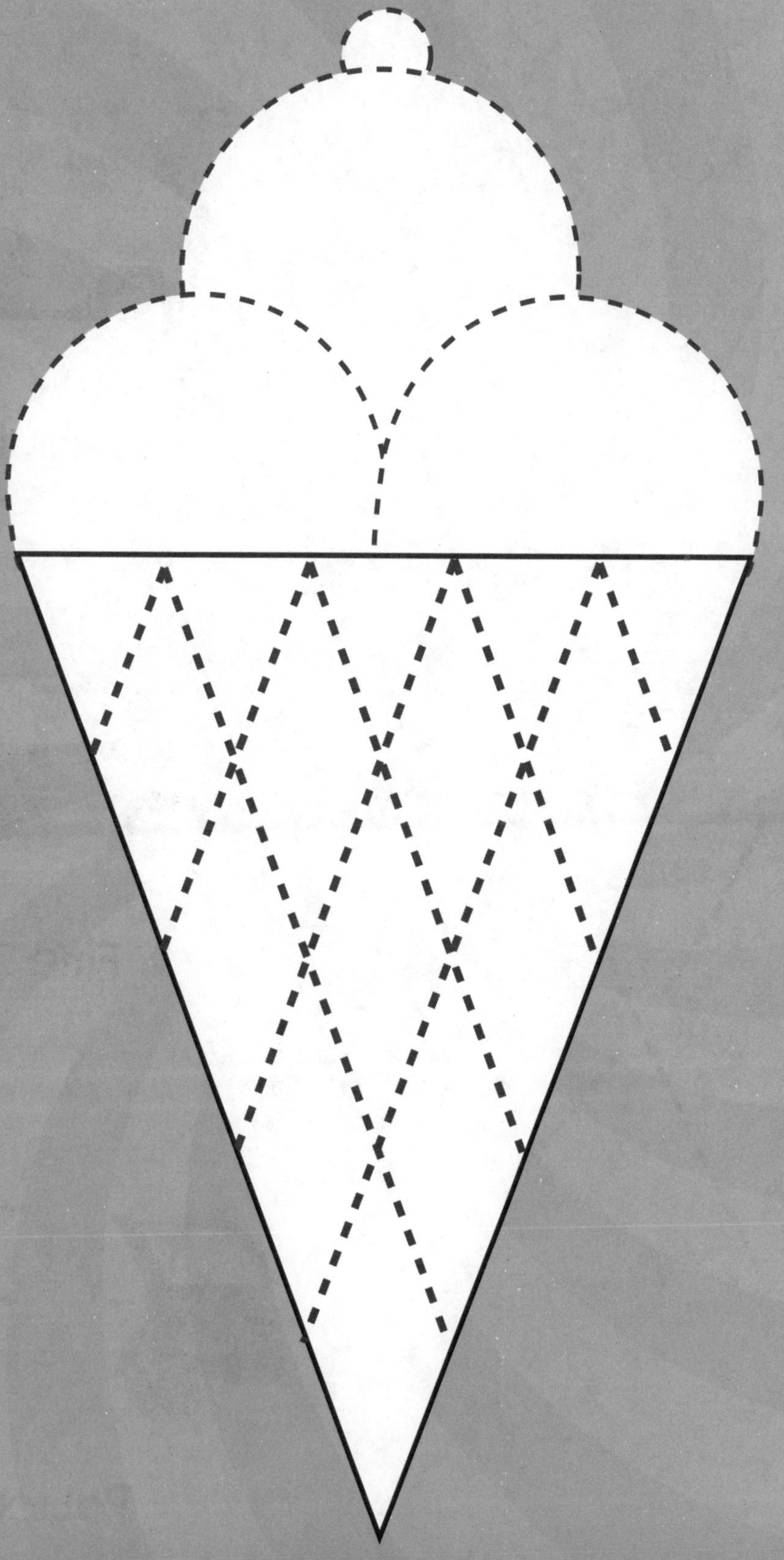

Emergency Helpers

Help the emergency helpers reach their vehicles.

Travel Buddies

Help the travel buddies reach their vehicles.

Pilot

Airplane

Captain

Ship

Driver

Taxi

Balloon Race

Trace the lines on the hot air balloons and complete the picture.

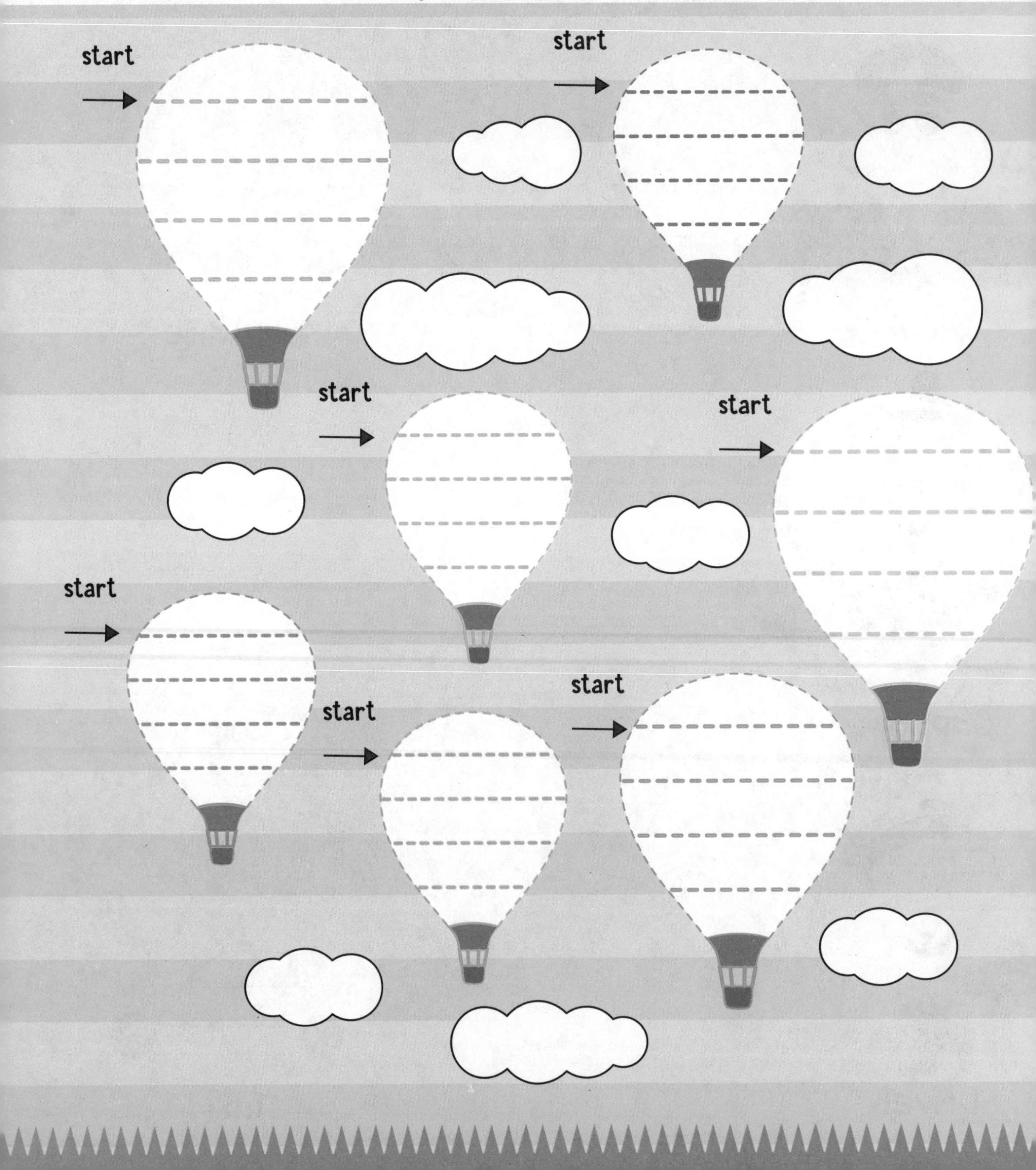

Balloon Strings

Trace the balloon strings and complete the picture.

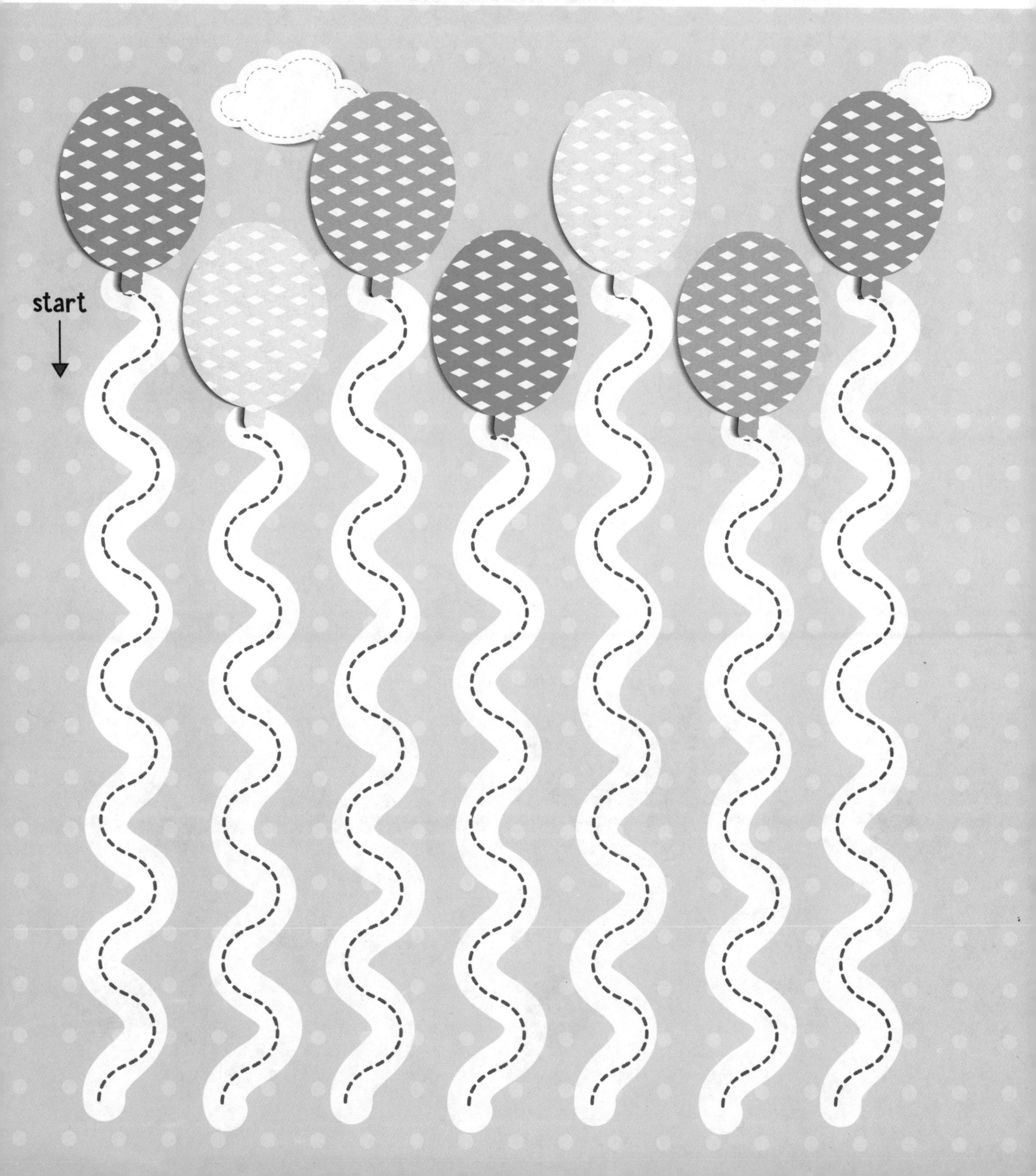

A Winding Way

Help the pirate find treasure by taking the correct path.